Sweet SCOTTISH FOLDS

UNIQUE! QUIET! GENTLE!

CALM! LOVABLE! RARE!

ABDO
Publishing Company

Katherine Hengel

Consulting Editor, Diane Craig, M.A./Reading Specialist

visit us at www.abdopublishing.com

Published by ABDO Publishing Company, a division of ABDO, P.O. Box 398166, Minneapolis, Minnesota 55439.

Printed in the United States of America, North Mankato, Minnesota
062011
092011

PRINTED ON RECYCLED PAPER

Editor: Liz Salzmann
Content Developer: Nancy Tuminelly
Cover and Interior Design and Production:
Anders Hanson, Mighty Media
Illustrations: Bob Doucet
Photo Credits: Shutterstock

Library of Congress Cataloging-in-Publication Data
Hengel, Katherine.
Sweet Scottish folds / authored by Katherine Hengel ; illustrated by Bob Doucet.
p. cm. -- (Cat craze set 2)
ISBN 978-1-61714-833-0
1. Scottish fold cat--Juvenile literature. I. Doucet, Bob, ill. II. Title.
SF449.S35H46 2012
636.8--dc22
2010053274

CONTENTS

The SCOTTISH FOLD

No other cat has ears like a Scottish fold! Their special ears fold forward. That's how they got their name. But their ears aren't all that is special about Scottish folds. They are very gentle, loving cats. They are great companions!

FACIAL FEATURES

Head

Scottish folds have round heads and short necks.

Muzzle

Scottish folds have short, wide **muzzles** with strong chins.

Eyes

Scottish folds have large, round eyes. Their faces look very cute and sweet!

Ears

Scottish folds have small ears. The ears fold forward and down.

BODY BASICS

Size

Adult Scottish folds weigh about 7 to 11 pounds (3 to 5 kg).

Build

Scottish folds are **medium-sized** cats. They have rounded, sturdy bodies.

Tail

A Scottish fold's tail is about as long as its body.

Legs and Feet

Scottish folds have short legs and round feet.

COAT & COLOR

Scottish Fold Fur

Scottish folds may be longhaired or shorthaired. The short coats are **dense** and soft. The fur sticks out from the body. It doesn't lay flat!

The long coats are very full around the face and tail. They even have tufts of hair on the tips of their ears! Both coat types come in many colors and patterns. Some Scottish folds are all white!

RED FUR

RED AND WHITE SHORTHAIR

Scottish folds come in many different colors and patterns. The photos on these pages show just a few examples.

HEALTH & CARE

Life Span

Scottish folds can live for 15 years or longer!

Health Concerns

Their folded ears are caused by a special **gene.** This gene can also cause some health problems. But Scottish folds from good **breeders** are usually very healthy.

VET'S CHECKLIST

- Have your Scottish fold spayed or neutered. This will prevent unwanted kittens.
- Visit a vet for regular checkups.
- Ask your vet which types of food and litter are right for your Scottish fold.
- Clean your Scottish fold's teeth and ears once a week.
- Ask your vet about shots that may benefit your cat.

ATTITUDE & BEHAVIOR

Personality

Scottish Folds are very sweet. They love their humans! Scottish folds are quiet and calm. They like to sleep on their backs with their legs sticking up! They are comfortable around dogs, children, and other cats.

Activity Level

Scottish folds are usually peaceful, but they can be active too. Some run and play more than others! Most of them are gentle and friendly.

All About Me

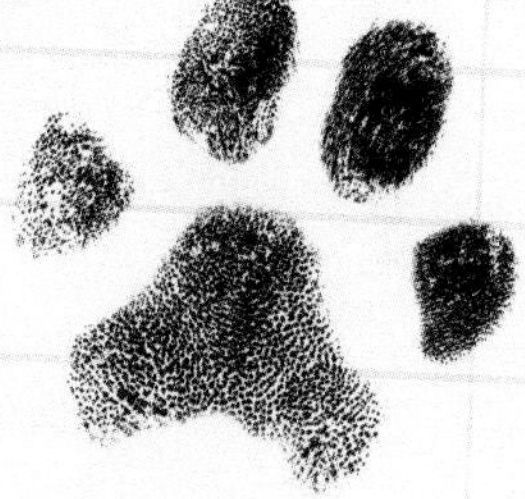

Hi! My name is Samson. I'm a Scottish fold. I just wanted to let you know a few things about me. I made some lists below of things I like and dislike. Check them out!

Things I Like

- Spending time with my family
- Sleeping on my back
- Cuddling with my owner
- Hanging out with other animals
- Following my owner around
- Playing with toys

Things I Dislike

- Being alone for a long time
- Not having any friends
- Getting bored

LITTERS & KITTENS

Litter Size

Female Scottish folds usually give birth to about five kittens.

Diet

Newborn kittens drink their mother's milk. They can begin to eat kitten food when they are about six weeks old. Kitten food is different from cat food. It has the extra **protein**, fat, **vitamins**, and **minerals** that kittens need to grow.

Growth

Scottish fold kittens are born with straight ears. After about three weeks, the ears of some of them fold. The other kittens grow up with straight ears.

Scottish fold kittens should stay with their mothers until they are two to three months old. Scottish folds are full grown when they are one year old.

BUYING A SCOTTISH FOLD

Choosing a Breeder

It's best to buy a kitten from a **breeder**, not a pet store. When you visit a cat breeder, ask to see the mother and father of the kittens. Make sure the parents are healthy, friendly, and well behaved.

Picking a Kitten

Choose a kitten that isn't too active or too shy. If you sit down, some of the kittens may come over to you. One of them might be the right one for you!

Is It the Right Cat for You?

Buying a cat is a big decision. You'll want to make sure your new pet suits your lifestyle.

Get out a piece of paper. Draw a line down the middle.

Read the statements listed here. Each time you agree with a statement from the left column, make a mark on the left side of your paper. When you agree with a statement from the right column, make a mark on the right side of your paper.

I want a very loving cat.	☐	☐	I like cats that can be by themselves.
Calm cats are the best.	☐	☐	Energetic cats are the best.
Folded ears look cute!	☐	☐	Ears that fold are kind of gross.
I would like a quiet cat.	☐	☐	I love it when cats meow a lot.

If you made more marks on the left side than on the right side, a Scottish fold may be the right cat for you! If you made more marks on the right side of your paper, you might want to consider another breed.

Some Things You'll Need

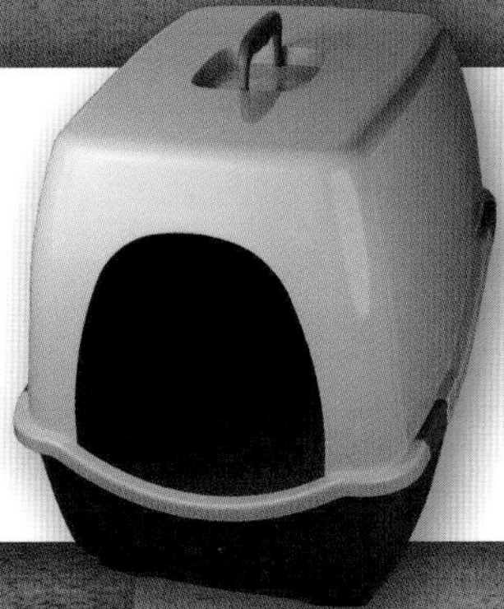

Cats go to the bathroom in a **litter box**. It should be kept in a quiet place. Most cats learn to use their litter box all by themselves. You just have to show them where it is! The dirty **litter** should be scooped out every day. The litter should be changed completely every week.

Your cat's **food and water dishes** should be wide and shallow. This helps your cat keep its whiskers clean. The dishes should be in a different area than the litter box. Cats do not like to eat and go to the bathroom in the same area.

Cats love to scratch! **Scratching posts** help keep cats from scratching the furniture. The scratching post should be taller than your cat. It should have a wide, heavy base so it won't tip over.

Cats are natural predators. Without small animals to hunt, cats may become bored and unhappy. **Cat toys** can satisfy your cat's need to chase and capture. They will help keep your cat entertained and happy.

Cats should not play with balls of yarn or string. If they accidentally eat the yarn, they could get sick.

Cat claws should be trimmed regularly with special cat claw **clippers**. Regular nail clippers will also work. Some people choose to have their cat's claws removed by a vet. But most vets and animal rights groups think declawing is cruel.

You should brush your cat regularly with a **cat hair brush**. This will help keep its coat healthy and clean.

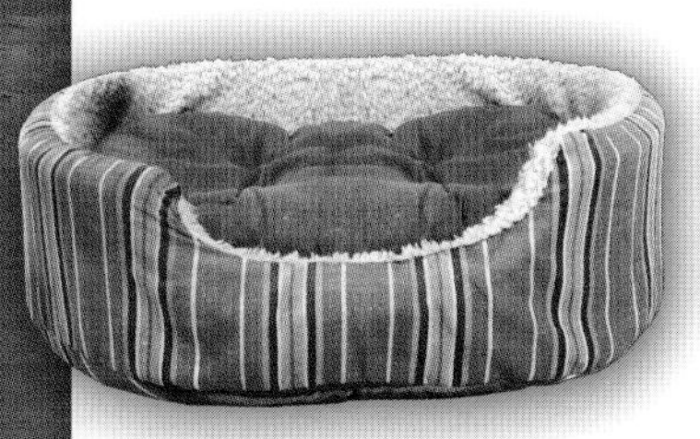

A **cat bed** will give your cat a safe, comfortable place to sleep.

LIVING WITH A SCOTTISH FOLD

Being a Good Companion

Scottish folds are not very **demanding.** They need good homes, healthy food, and a lot of love! They don't need a lot of **grooming.** Just brush your Scottish fold occasionally.

Inside or Outside?

It's a good idea to keep a Scottish fold inside. Most vets and **breeders** agree that it is best for cats to be kept inside. That way the cats are safe from predators and cars.

Feeding Your Scottish Fold

Scottish folds may be fed regular cat food. Your vet can help you choose the best food for your cat.

Cleaning the Litter Box

Like all cats, Scottish folds like to be clean. They don't like smelly or dirty litter boxes. If the litter box is dirty, they may go to the bathroom somewhere else. Ask your vet for advice if your cat isn't using its box.

DANGER: POISONOUS FOODS

Some people like to feed their cats table scraps. Here are some human foods that can make cats sick.

TOMATOES

POTATOES

ONIONS

GARLIC

CHOCOLATE

GRAPES

FIRST SUSIE, THEN SNOOKS!

In 1961, a Scottish shepherd noticed a special cat on his neighbor's farm. The barn cat's name was Susie. Susie was white and had very special ears that folded forward! The shepherd thought Susie was wonderful. He asked if he could have one of her kittens.

A year later, Susie had a litter of kittens. Two of them had folded ears. The shepherd and his wife adopted one. It was an all-white female. They named her Snooks. All Scottish folds are **related** to Susie and Snooks!

FIND THE SCOTTISH FOLD

A

B

C

D

Answers: **A)** American curl **B)** Russian blue **C)** Oriental shorthair **D)** Scottish fold (correct)

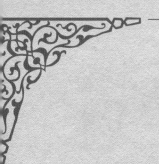

THE SCOTTISH FOLD QUIZ

1. Scottish folds are very gentle, loving cats. **True or false?**
2. Scottish fold ears fold forward and down. **True or false?**
3. Scottish folds are never all white. **True or false?**
4. Scottish folds like to sleep on their backs. **True or false?**
5. Scottish folds are born with straight ears. **True or false?**
6. A Scottish shepherd noticed Susie in a city. **True or false?**

Answers: **1)** true **2)** true **3)** false **4)** true **5)** true **6)** false

GLOSSARY

breed - a group of animals or plants with common ancestors. A *breeder* is someone whose job is to breed certain animals or plants.

demanding - needing a lot of time or attention.

dense - thick or crowded together.

gene - part of a cell in the body that is passed from parents to their children.

groom - to clean the fur of an animal.

medium-sized - not the largest or the smallest.

mineral - a natural element that plants, animals, and people need to be healthy.

muzzle - the nose and jaws of an animal.

protein - a substance found in all plant and animal cells.

related - part of the same family.

vitamin - a substance needed for good health, found naturally in plants and meats.